The Guide To Home Canning

Compiled by:
Ed & Linda Yoder Pattin
9193 Winesburg Road
Dundee, Ohio 44624
(330) 359-7174

Typeset And Printed By:

2881 State Route 93 ● Sugarcreek, Ohio 44681
(330) 852-4687 ● Fax (330) 852-2689
Toll-Free ● 1-888-406-BOOK (2665)

Table Of Contents

✓ Abbreviations ✓

c. = cup	gal. = gallon
t. = teaspoon	pkg. = packages
T. = tablespoon	oz. = ounces
qt. = quart	lb. = pounds
sm. = small	min. = minutes
lg. = large	med. = medium

Basic Canning

Items Needed For Canning:

Pressure Cooker or boiling Water Canner
Glass Jars, Mason or Ball
Jar Lifter
Lids and Rings
Ladle
Canning Funnel
Food Mill or Victorio Strainer
Timer
Large Saucepot

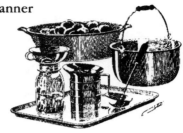

Canning:

Always check jars for nicks, cracks, uneven rims, or other defects. Wash jars with hot soapy water and rinse. Fill with food, then always wipe rim before putting on lids. Heat lids in hot water on stove, put on jars, and screw rings on tightly. Then cold pack.

Cold Packing & Water Bath:

Put lids and rings on, put in canner and cover with water. Bring to a boil for whatever time the recipe recommends.

Cold Packing Times:

Chicken - 3 hours
Hamburger - 2 hours
Fried Steak - 1 hour
Spare Ribs - 3 hours
Cherries - 15 minutes
Peaches - 15 minutes
Sweet Corn - 3 hours
Green Beans - 3 hours

Young Roosters - 2 hours
Beef Chunks - 3 hours
Fried Pork Chops - 1 hour
Sausage - 1½ hours
Pears - 15 minutes
Raspberries - 10 minutes

Checking For Sealing:

After jars have cooled, check lids for seal by pressing on the center of each lid. If the center of the lid is pulled down and does not pop, remove rings and try to lift the lid off with your fingers. If lid does not flex and you cannot lift it off, the lid has a good vacumn seal. Wipe lid and jar surface with warm soapy dishcloth and then dry with dish towel. Label and store in cool dark place.

God Has Blessed America

Our country, God has richly blessed
With food and eats, so many,
So that it might be referred to as:
"The land of milk and honey."

But did we ever stop to think
Not all lands have such wealth?
Some may be quite hungry
Not food enough for health.

While for our meals, we serve so much
Rich foods we like to taste,
Then for our health it is not good
And perhaps some goes to waste.

Might we not displease our Lord
Serving more than for our good?
Or would we show our thankfulness
By decorating food!

God has given; God could take!
It's all within His power;
We know not at all, what might befall
Within a coming hour.

Someday, we might be made
To think back to our past,
If all the foods we wasted
We then could only grasp!

Yes, God has blessed America
So let us try with prayer
To use the blessings rightfully
And with the needy share.

Canning Meats

BEEF STEW

5 lbs. stew meat
12 c. potatoes, cubed
8 c. carrots in ½ inch slices

3 c. chopped celery
3 c. chopped onion
salt and pepper to taste

Boil meat in water until tender, add vegetables and seasonings. Bring to boil. Put in jars, seal, and cold pack for 1½ hours.

CANNING BEEF STEAKS

1 c. brown sugar
1 c. salt

1 gal. water

Mix together and put 1 cup of this brine in each qt. jar and fill with steaks. Seal; cold pack 2 hours. Makes 15 qt. When serving use brine to make gravy.

CANNED HAMBURGER PATTIES

15 lbs. hamburger
4 eggs
4 slices bread
2 c. rolled oats
72 soda crackers
6 c. milk
½ c. salt
2 t. pepper

Sauce:
1½ qt. catsup
3 onions, diced
2 T. Worcestershire sauce
1 T. mustard
½ c. brown sugar
1 T. seasoning salt

This is enough to fill 14 qt. - ¾ full. Make your patties, roll in flour, and brown in skillet. Cold pack for 2 hours.

CANNED HOTDOGS OR BOLOGNA

Place in quart jars, fill to neck with water. Seal and cold pack for 1½ hours.

SAUSAGE

fresh smoked sausage in casing

Cut sausage in desired length. Put in wide mouth jars, fill to neck with water. Seal and cold pack for 3 hours.

SAUSAGE OR HAMBURGER

ground sausage or hamburger
   Fry meat, add Lawry's salt, pepper, and salt to taste. Put in jars and add ¼ c. water to each quart. Seal and cold pack for 1½ hours.

BEEF CHUNKS

   Fill jar with beef chunks, put ½ t. salt on top, then seal and cold pack for 3 hours. Good for beef-n-noodles, barbecue beef sandwiches, stew, etc.

FRIED STEAK OR PORK CHOPS

fresh ¼" thick round steak, cut into 3" to 4" pieces
   Roll steaks in flour and fry in butter, season and put in jars. Add ¼ c. water to each quart jar. Seal and cold pack for 1 hour.

CANNED MEAT LOAF

15 lbs. hamburger	**3 c. water**
7 slices bread, crumbled	**pepper to taste**
36 white cracker squares, crushed	**½ c. salt**
1 c. oatmeal	**4 eggs**

   Mix well. Pack in jars. Cold pack 4 hours. Can be eaten cold, sliced from jar or heated.

CANNED HAMBURGER

15 lbs. hamburger	**Sauce:**
4 eggs	**3 T. Worcestershire sauce**
4 slices bread, cubed	**9 T. vinegar**
1 c. rolled oats	**6 T. brown sugar**
36 crackers	**3 c. catsup**
3 c. water (some milk)	**1½ c. tomato juice**
½ c. salt	**¾ c. chopped onion**

   Mix first 7 items and make into small patties or balls and fry. Put in wide mouth jars. Mix sauce and pour over meat until jars are ¾ full. Cold pack 1½ to 2 hours. Very good and handy to have.

MEAT BALLS WITH SAUCE

15 lbs. hamburger	1 T. Worcestershire sauce
4 eggs	2 T. brown sugar
4 slices bread	3 T. vinegar
1 c. oatmeal	1 c. ketchup
36 soda crackers	½ c. tomato juice
3 c. water	6 T. chopped onion
½ c. salt	

Mix well the first 7 ingredients. Make small balls and fry. Place in jars. Mix rest of ingredients and put in jars until ¾ full. Cold pack for 1½ hours.

MEAT BALLS

10 lbs. hamburger	pepper, salt, Lawry's salt to
3 eggs	taste
3 c. Italian bread crumbs	chopped onions (opt.)

Mix together. Form 1 inch balls. Put on cookie sheets and bake at 350° for ½ hour, or until done. Put in jars. Add about 2 in. water, seal and cold pack for 1½ hours. Serve warm with mashed potatoes and gravy. Very good.

GROUND CHICKEN BALLS

20 lbs. ground chicken	Lawry's salt, pepper, and
6 c. bread crumbs	garlic salt to taste
4 eggs	

Mix together, make balls and bake on cookie sheets at 400° for 20 to 30 min. Put in jars and add ½ c. water. Seal and cold pack for 1½ hours. Open and add water and 1 can cream of mushroom soup, heat. Very good.

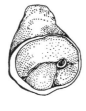

CANNED MEAT BALLS WITH GRAVY

10 lbs. ground beef	¼ c. salt
4 c. oatmeal	pepper to taste
4 c. milk	2 T. mustard
1 c. ketchup	½ t. oregano
3 eggs	½ t. sage
1 sm. onion, chopped	2 T. Lawry's salt

Mix thoroughly. Wet hands for easier handling to form into balls. Fry the balls then make thin brown gravy to pour over meat balls in jars. Cold pack for 2 hours or pressure 1 hour and 25 min. at 10 lbs. pressure. Serve with mashed potatoes.

CANNED CHICKEN BREAST
boneless chicken breast
salt

Wash chicken breast, put in jars and put 1 t. salt on top. Clean off rim and put on lids and rings. Cold pack for 3 hours. Use for chicken salad or roll in flour and brown in oil and butter.

CHICKEN CHUNKS AND BROTH
chickens   Salt

Type of chickens: stewing hens, roasters, or capons. Cut up chicken and boil in water. Add 1 T. salt. Boil until tender, remove from water. Save water to use as broth. Cool chicken and pick off bones. Cut into chunks and put into jars. Put broth in; enough to cover chicken. Clean off rims and put on lids and rings. Cold pack for 3 hours. Put extra broth in pint jars and cold pack for 2½ hours.

CURING HAMS AND BACON (COUNTRY STYLE)

100 lb. ham
10 lbs. salt
2 lbs. brown sugar
2 oz. salt petre

1 oz. red pepper
about 4 gal. water, just
enough to cover ham

First, rub the hams with common salt and lay them into the tub. Then take the above ingredients and put them into a vessel over the fire and heat it hot, stirring it often. Remove all scum, and allow it to boil for 10 min. Let cool and then pour over the meat. After laying in this brine 5-6 weeks, take out, drain and wipe. Then smoke with hickory from 2-3 weeks. Pieces of side meat or bacon may remain in the pickle for 2 weeks which should be sufficient.

Canning Soups

VEGETABLE SOUP

5 lg. bags frozen mixed vegetables
1 or 2 qts. beef chunks
½ c. white sugar
½ gal. celery, diced
½ gal. onions, diced

3 cans beef broth (46 oz.)
2 cans V-8 juice (46 oz.)
4 c. potatoes, diced
8 t. beef bouillon

Cook mixed vegetables, celery, onions, potatoes, and chunks separately until tender. Mix together. Add juices from boiling meat and vegetables. Boil slowly until well blended. Cold pack for 2 hours.

CHUNKY BEEF SOUP

21 qts. water
1 c. beef mix or bouillon
2 lg. cans beef broth
2 lg. onions
¼ c. salt
3 qt. green beans
4 qt. tomato juice

2 c. white sugar
4 c. flour
5 lbs. hamburger, seasoned
and fried
4 qt. carrots
4 qt. potatoes
3 pt. peas

Thicken water, beef mix, beef broth, onions, salt, tomato juice, and sugar with the flour. Chunk the vegetables. Salt and cook until tender. Add hamburger and mix all together. Put in jars and cold pack for 3 hours. Or pressure cook for 1½ hours. Makes about 20 qts.

VEGGIE AND BEEF SOUP

12 ears corn cut off the cobs
2 sm. heads cabbage, shredded
½ bushel tomatoes, juiced
12 carrots, diced
12 onions, diced

3 stalks celery
yellow & green beans, as
desired
5 lbs. meat of your choice,
hamburger, or beef
chunks, must be cooked

Precook vegetables separately. Mix together and add alphabet macaroni to thicken as desired precooked. Put in jars and cold pack for 3 hours. Makes 13 qts.

VEGETABLE SOUP

1 qt. potatoes
1 qt. carrots
1 qt. celery
1 qt. pork & beans
2 c. onions
3 qt. tomato juice
2 lbs. hamburger, fried

1 beef roast, cubed
2 qt. beef broth
2 t. chili powder
½ c. sugar
salt & pepper to taste
2 cans beans with bacon
 soup

Put all ingredients in kettle, cook for ½ hour. Put in jars and cold pack for 3 hours.

VEGETABLE SOUP

2 qts. tomato juice
4 qts. beef broth
4 c. roast
4 c. potatoes, cubed
4 c. carrots, cubed
2 c. green beans

2 c. corn
2 c. peas
1 c. onions, chopped
1 c. celery, chopped
1 t. pepper
2 t. salt
½ t. garlic powder

Cook roast for 3 hours in water and seasonings, pepper, salt, garlic powder, and Lawry's seasoning salt. Cut in small chunks. Put all ingredients in 12 qt. kettle. Bring to a boil and then simmer for 1 hour. Thicken with flour and water mixture. Put in jars and cold pack for 2½ hours.

CHICKEN NOODLE SOUP

8 qts. broth
2 qts. potatoes
2 qts. carrots
1 qt. peas
1 qt. green beans
2 c. onions, chopped
3 c. celery, chopped

½ c. chopped parsley
2 qts. chicken chunks
¾ c. chicken soup base
salt and pepper to taste
10 qts. water
2 (8 oz.) pkg. Inn Maid
 med. Noodles

Put all ingredients in lg. kettle. Bring to a boil, then add noodles. Simmer for 1 hour. Put in jars and cold pack for 2½ hours.

CHILI SOUP

5 c. tomato puree
5 c. tomato juice
6 c. kidney beans
1½ c. brown sugar
6 lbs. hamburger, browned

1 lg. onion
2 heaping T. flour
chili powder, salt, pepper,
 and red pepper to taste
garlic (opt.)

Put all together in a big kettle. Bring to a boil, then put in jars and cold pack for 2½ hours.

CHILI SOUP

12 lbs. hamburger
3 lg. onions
1½ gal. tomato juice
1½ gal. kidney beans or chili beans

1 pt. homemade catsup
3 c. brown sugar
4 T. chili powder

Fry together beef and onions. Add 2 c. flour and stir, add rest of ingredients. Then add enough water to make 5 gals. soup. Simmer 1 hour then put in jars and cold pack for 1½ hours. Very easy. Good over baked potatoes with cheddar cheese.

TOMATO SOUP

1 peck tomatoes
1 bunch celery
3 lg. onions
1 lg. handful fresh parsley

1 c. flour
1 c. white sugar
water

Chop and boil first 4 ingredients until soft. Put through Victorio strainer or seive. Then mix together flour and sugar. Mix well. Add enough water to dissolve then stir into juice. Put in jars and cold pack for 25 min.

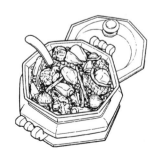

LIKE CAMPBELLS TOMATO SOUP

½ c. chopped onion   ¾ c. sugar
1½ c. oleo   1½ t. pepper
2¼ c. flour   7 to 8 qt. tomato juice
¼ c. salt

Saute onion in oleo. Stir in flour, salt, sugar, and pepper. Cook until smooth and bubbly, stirring constantly. Remove from heat, gradually stir in tomato juice. Bring to a boil, stirring constantly. Boil 1 min. Fill jars and cold pack for 30 min. To serve mix in equal amounts of milk.

BEAN AND BACON SOUP

4 lbs. dried Great Northern Beans   2 t. pepper
2 lbs. bacon   8 c. potatoes
4 c. onions   5 qt. tomato juice
5 c. celery   2 bay leaves
4 c. carrots   salt to taste

Soak beans overnight, then cook until soft. Cook potatoes, carrots, and celery until soft. Cut bacon fine and fry. Remove bacon and cook onions in grease until soft. Put all ingredients together in canner and heat until it simmers. Remove bay leaves before putting in jars. Cold pack 1 hour in pressure or 2 hours in water bath. Makes 15 quarts.

BEAN AND BACON

2 lbs. dried Navy beans, soaked overnight
3 c. chopped onions   2 lbs. bacon
2 c. diced celery   2 c. diced potatoes
2½ c. tomato juice   2 c. sliced carrots
2 bay leaves   1 t. pepper

Cook Navy beans until soft. Cook together onions, potatoes, and carrots until soft. Fry bacon and crumble in small pieces. Add bacon drippings and bacon. Simmer for 15 min., then cold pack for 3 hours or pressure can for 75 min. at 10 lbs. pressure.

BEAN & HAM SOUP

4 lbs. Navy beans, cooked in 12 qts. water

3 lbs. ham, cubed
2 c. chopped onion
8 c. mashed potatoes
4 c. diced celery

4 c. diced carrots
2 qt. tomato juice
16 t. salt
2 t. pepper

Put all together in kettle, simmer for ½ hour. Put in jars, cold pack for 3 hours or pressure cook for 1 hour. Makes 14 qts.

Canning Sauces

CATSUP

½ bushel tomatoes   6 lg. onions

Boil and put through cloth, add: 1½ c. vinegar, 4 c. brown sugar, 3 c. white Karo, and spices. Cold pack for 5 min.

KETCHUP

1 peck tomatoes   1 c. vinegar
3 peppers   1 T. salt
4 big onions, chopped   3 c. white sugar
       1½ T. ketchup spice

Cook first 3 ingredients until soft. Pour in colander or cloth, a clean pillow case works good. Pour juice in and tie with small rope; hang up for 3 hours. Throw away juice and use pulp. Add last 4 ingredients. Cook until thickened. Then add 1 t. tumeric and 1 T. cornstarch. Put into jars, seal and cold pack for 15 min.

SPAGHETTI SAUCE

6 to 10 lb. hamburger   2 c. sugar
1½ T. pepper   3 onions, chopped
3 T. garlic salt   3 peppers
6 T. parsley flakes   3 sm. cans mushrooms
6 T. butter   ½ c. cooking oil
3 (12 oz.) cans tomato paste   2 jars (med. or lg.) Ragu
3 cans water   spaghetti sauce
6 qt. tomato juice
3 T. salt

Brown the first 5 ingredients; then combine with the remaining 10 ingredients. Cook 1 hour. Put in jars and cold pack for 2 hours. Makes 13 quarts. Watch closely because it burns easily.

PIZZA SAUCE

15 c. tomato juice   1 c. Wesson oil
3 onions   6 - 7 T. flour
3 t. oregano   2 (12 oz.) cans tomato
2 t. black pepper   paste
1½ c. white sugar

Mix all together and bring to a boil. Put in jars and cold pack for 30 min.

CATSUP

1 gal. tomato juice	1 T. salt
1 T. ground mustard	1 c. vinegar
1 t. black pepper	3 c. sugar
1 T. allspice	¼ t. garlic salt

Boil down to half amount or to desired thickness. Put in jars and seal while hot.

PIZZA & SPAGHETTI SAUCE

3 med. onions, cut fine	3 (6 oz.) cans tomato paste
1 c. white sugar	5 cans tomato soup
1 t. garlic salt	3 qts. tomato juice
2 T. oregano leaves	2 green peppers
1 - 2 cans mushroom soup	

Dice green peppers and cook in tomato juice. Put everything in a big bowl and stir together. Put in jars and cold pack for 30 min. Makes 12 pts. or 6 qts.

PIZZA SAUCE

1 c. cooking oil	1½ c. white sugar
1 T. basil	½ t. salt
1 T. oregano	

Cook half bushel tomatoes. Chop 5 onions and add 4 hot peppers to tomatoes. Cook to soup stage for 2½ hours. Then run through sieve. Add whats listed up above. Cook another hour, then add 4 (12 oz.) cans tomato paste. Bring to a boil. Pack in jars and seal.

PIZZA SAUCE

½ bushel tomatoes
2 green bell peppers
3 lbs. onions
3 hot peppers
6 bay leaves
8 (6 oz.) cans tomato paste
2 whole garlic, sliced thin

1 pt. salad oil
1½ c. sugar
½ c. salt
2 T. oregano
2 T. parsley flakes
2 T. basil

Cut up tomatoes, peppers, and onions. Put in blender. Put all together and cook for 1 hour. After cooking 1 hour, add rest of ingredients and cook another hour. Remove bay leaves and pour into hot jars and seal.

HEINZ CATSUP

1½ gal. strained tomatoes
2 T. salt
1 T. pickle spice
1 T. dry mustard

3 T. corn starch
3½ c. white vinegar
2 onions in a cloth bag

½ t. red pepper (Put above 3 ingredients in cloth bag)

Cook together tomatoes and salt. Put in cloth bag: pickle spice, mustard, pepper, and onions. Put into tomato mixture and cook for 2 hours on low heat, remove bag then add cornstarch and vinegar. Mix well. Put in jars and cold pack for 30 min.

PIZZA SAUCE

2 onions, cut fine
1 c. white sugar
1 t. garlic salt
1 can mushroom soup

3 sm. cans tomato paste
3 lb. can tomato soup
3 qts. tomato juice

Mix all together and put in jars. Cold pack for 30 min. Makes 12 qts.

MEXICAN TOMATO SAUCE

24 lbs. tomatoes
6 med. onions
6 lg. carrots
8 med. peppers
4 sticks celery
6 hot peppers
¼ c. olive oil
1 to 2 bulbs garlic

½ c. salt
4 T. oregano
6 T. basil
3 T. chili powder
cilantro to taste
cumin to taste
1 (10 oz.) tomato paste

Put tomatoes in blender or food processor until liquified. Chop fine, onions, carrots, peppers, celery, and hot peppers. Saute in olive oil; add garlic bulbs, minced. Then add salt, oregano, basil, chili powder, cilantro, cumin, and red pepper to taste. Mix, then add tomato paste. Cook everything together for 2 hours; then pour into jars and cold pack for 45 min. Use for spaghetti, Spanish rice, or pizza.

SPAGHETTI SAUCE

½ bushel tomatoes, cut in chunks
5 onions, chopped fine
2 T. oregano

3 bay leaves
1½ c. sugar
2 (12 oz.) cans tomato paste

Cook together tomatoes, onions, oregano, and bay leaves really well. Put through sieve. Add sugar, salt, and pepper. Cook for ½ hour. Add tomato paste; cook for 15 min. more, then add clear jell enough to thicken to desired thickness. Put in jars and cold pack for 1 hour.

Canning
Vegetables

CANNED SWEET CORN

Fill qt. jars loosely with sweet corn. Do not pack. To each jar add:

1 T. lemon juice (Realemon)   1 t. salt
1 t. sugar

Fill with water as usual. Cook in pressure cooker under 10 lbs. pressure for 10-15 min. This sweet corn tastes almost like fresh corn when opened. We had no problem with it going sour.

CORN (FOR FREEZING)

corn, cut off of cob   salt
water   white sugar
butter or margarine

To each 8 cups of cut off corn, add 1 c. water, 1 stick butter or margarine, 1 T. salt, and 1 T. sugar. Simmer on low heat for 5 min. Stir to keep from sticking. Pour into large bowl. Cool on ice and put into containers to freeze. Very good!

POTATOES AND CARROTS

potatoes   salt
carrots   water

Peel and cut potatoes in small chunks. Wash and brush carrots and cut up. Fill pint jars half full with carrots and fill rest of jar up with potatoes. Put ½ t. salt on top. Fill jar with water. Put on lids and rings. Cold pack for 3 hours. Use for soups, pot pies, or dumplings.

PEAS

peas

Put peas in boiling water for 2 min. Drain and put into jars. Fill with water and ½ t. salt per qt. jar. Seal and cold pack for 3 hours.

CANNING POTATOES

When you dig potatoes this fall, pick up all small ones. Scrub them nice and clean; leave skin on. Fill pt. jars with potatoes. Fill with water and cold pack for 3 hours. Very handy to add to meat or vegetables, or drain and fry in pan and top with cheese or sour cream.

CANNED CORN

1 pt. corn	**1 T. flour**
2 T. butter	**½ T. sugar**

Cut corn off of cob, whole kernel, do not scrape. Add water to wash all milk off of corn. A lot of silk pieces, etc. will float to the top. Remove these. Wash and drain at least 3 times. Fill jars; add salt and cold water. Put lids on and cold pack for 3 hours. To serve, melt butter in sauce pan, add flour and sugar. Stir until blended. Add corn along with liquid. Heat to just boiling and serve. Boiling too long spoils the flavor.

CANNING SWEET POTATOES

Peel and cut sweet potatoes. Pack in jars. Cover with syrup made with **1 c. white sugar and 2 c. water.** Put lids on and cold pack for 1 hour.

RED BEETS

red beets   **salt**

Wash beets well, cook with skins on until tender. Then slip skins under cold water. Save beet juice. Chop beets up in desired size. Put in jars, fill ½ full beet juice and the rest with water. Add dash of salt to each jar. Seal and cold pack for 15 min. Serve warm with butter and salt. Good side dish.

CANNED CARROTS

Wash and peel carrots. Cut into slices and put into jars. Add ¼ t. salt and fill rest of jar with water. Seal and cold pack for 3 hours. Good side dish. Open, heat and add butter and salt.

CANNING RED BEETS

beets, leave about 4" of tops
2 c. sugar
2 c. water
2 c. vinegar

1 t. cinnamon
1 t. cloves
1 t. allspice

Cook beets until soft. When soft, peel and cut into pieces. Make syrup of all ingredients. Add salt. Simmer for 15 min. Put into hot jars and seal. Cold pack for 15 min.

GREEN BEANS

beans
water

Use green or yellow beans. Wash and cut in 1 inch pieces. Put in jars; fill with water. Cold pack for 3 hours.

CALICO BEANS

2 lbs. bacon
4 lbs. hamburger
4 cans kidney beans
4 cans Pork-n-Beans
2 cans butter beans

2 pkgs. frozen baby limas
4 c. brown sugar
4 c. ketchup
8 t. mustard
8 T. vinegar

Fry meat and drain. Put all together and put into jars. Cold pack for 2 hours.

DELICIOUS BARBECUE BEANS

2 qt. baby lima beans, cooked
2 qt. soup beans, cooked
2 qt. red kidney beans, cooked
2 qt. pea beans, cooked
1 qt. chopped sweet pickles

1 stalk celery, cut up
6 lg. onions
1 bottle barbecue sauce
tomato juice as needed

Add **brown sugar** to taste. Then add **salt, ¼ c. vinegar, 1 c. clear Karo, 2 c. flour to thicken.** Mix everything together. Put in jars and cold pack for 2 hours.

PORK-N-BEANS

8 lbs. Navy beans	4 qt. tomato juice
5 lbs. ham, cut fine	1½ bottle catsup (26 oz.)
1/3 c. salt	½ t. red pepper
3 c. water	1 t. dry mustard
3 c. white sugar	1 t. cinnamon
4 c. brown sugar	1 lg. onion, diced

Soak beans overnight. Cook until almost soft. Pour off water and add other ingredients. Fry onions and ham adding grease and all. Cold pack for 3 hours.

TO CAN NAVY BEANS

dried navy beans   **salt**

Soak beans overnight in water. Fill jars ¾ full and add dash of salt. Fill with hot water. Cold pack for 3 hours.

SAUERKRAUT

Shred cabbage like slaw. Press tight in quart jars with boiling water. For 1 quart, add **2 t. vinegar, 1 t. salt, and 1 t. white sugar**. Cover and let set for 6 weeks. Then cold pack for 30 min.

CROCK KRAUT

cabbage   **salt**

Shred cabbage as desired. For every 4 c. cabbage add 1½ T. salt. Mix all together and put 8 c. into crock. Stamp down until juice covers cabbage. Then add more cups. Do this until crock is ½ to ¾ full. Put water in garbage bag and put on top of cabbage to seal. Let set in room temperature for 6 weeks. Put in jars and cold pack for 15 min.

CORN SALAD

40 ears corn, cut off
½ c. salt
4 sweet peppers, red or green
2 bunches celery
2 head cabbage
3½ c. sugar

1 T. mustard
2 T. cornstarch
1 T. tumeric
1½ qt. vinegar
2 c. water
6 med. onions, chopped

Chop all fine, and mix together. Boil 10 min. stirring constantly. Put in jars, seal and cold pack for 1 hour.

Canning Fruits

APRICOTS

apricots   sugar
water

Wash apricots, cut in half. Pit but do not peel. Put in jars. 1 c. sugar to 3 c. water or more sugar if you desire. Bring to boiling point, pour over apricots in jars. Wipe off rims; put lids and rings on. Cold pack for 30 min.

CANNED PINEAPPLE

pineapples   Syrup:
                                            1 c. sugar & 3 c. water

Select nice ripe pineapples, wash them after twisting off green top. Cut them like you would a melon. Peel off peelings and cut out core. Now cut them in chunks or however you like them. A salsa master makes very nice crushed pineapple. Put them in pint jars and put syrup on them till covered. If your pineapple have enough juice to cover you don't have to add syrup. Boil in hot water bath for 10 min. after putting on flats and rings.

PEARS

pears   unsweetened pineapple
sugar   juice
water

Peel and cut pears into desired size. Put into jars. Bring to boiling 8 c. pineapple juice, 2 c. water, and 9 c. sugar. Pour over pears and seal. Cold pack for 15 min.

CHERRIES

cherries   Syrup:
                                            10 c. water & 8 c. sugar

Remove stones from cherries if desired, put in jars. Boil sugar and water. Fill jars with syrup. Seal and cold pack for 15 min.

APPLESAUCE

Cortland, Yellow Delicious, Banana, Smokehouse, Mckintosh, or your favorite kind of apples. Quarter and core apples, put in 12 qt. kettle and add **1 qt. water**. Cook until apples are soft and put through Victoria strainer. Add **sugar** to taste and put in jars. Seal and cold pack for 15 min.

FRUIT MIX

8 qt. watermelon
8 qt. muskmelon

8 qt. peaches
1 gal. pineapple chunks

Mix all together and put in jars. Cold pack for 15 min.

CANNING STRAWBERRIES

7 qt. crushed strawberries
4 c. sugar
5 T. clear jel

1 c. strawberry jello
3 c. water

Mix strawberries and sugar; set aside. Cook together jello, clear jel, and water. Add to strawberries. Put in jars and cold pack for 10 min. Let set in canning water until cool.

FRUIT COCKTAIL

1 bushel peaches
1 bushel pears
2 gal. pineapple tidbits
10 lbs. green grapes needed
maraschino cherries (opt.)

Syrup:
6 c. sugar
8 c. water
add more water if

Mix together and add syrup; mix well. Put in jars and seal; cold pack for 15 min. Makes 50 quarts.

PEACHES

peaches

sugar

Peel peaches and cut into chunks. Add white sugar until sweet enough. Put in jars and cold pack for 20 min. Add water if using Baby Gold peaches.

CANNED APPLE PIE FILLING

12 c. grated apples
5 c. white sugar
3 c. water
6 T. minute tapioca

Topping for Apple Pie:
1 c. quick rolled oats
1/3 c. firmly packed brown
  sugar
1/3 t. cinnamon
1/3 t. melted oleo or butter

Fill jars but not too full, with filling. Cold pack for 15 min. When ready to use, pour canned pie filling into BAKED pie shell. Sprinkle crumbs over top and bake for 10 min.

OLD FASHIONED MINCE MEAT

3 qts. chopped apples, not peeled
1 lb. raisins, cooked
½ c. water
½ c. cider or vinegar

4 qts. cooked beef
2½ t. cinnamon
2½ t. allspice
3½ c. brown sugar

Mix all together and cook until hot. Put the hot mixture in jars and cold pack for 25 min. Makes 8 qts. One quart makes 2 pies.

APPLE PIE FILLING

6 lbs. tart apples
4½ c. sugar
1 c. corn starch
2 t. cinnamon

¼ t. ground nutmeg
3 T. lemon juice
2 - 3 drops yellow food
  coloring

Blend together sugar, cornstarch, spices, and 1 t. salt. Stir in 10 c. water. Cook and stir until bubbly. Add Lemon juice and food coloring. Add apples and put in hot jars leaving ½" head space. Seal, process in boiling water bath for 20 min. Makes 6 quarts.

PEACH PIE FILLING

3 c. pineapple juice
3 c. water
6 c. white sugar

1½ c. water mixed with
1¾ c. Sure Jel

Boil 1st three ingredients, the glaze will be very thick. Then add the Sure Jel mixture slowly stirring all the time. Cook until thickened. Then peel and slice 6 quarts of peaches and add to glaze. Put in jars and cold pack for 15 min. Makes 7 quarts.

MINCEMEAT

4 lbs. beef meat
3 lbs. suet
3 lbs. brown sugar
3 lbs. currants
3 lbs. raisins
9 lbs. apples
½ lb. citron

½ lb. candied orange peel
¼ lb. candied lemon peel
4 oranges
2 lemons
1 oz. each mase, nutmeg,
   cinnamon, and cloves
3 qt. cider

Cover meat with water and cook until tender. Cut fine, but do not force down the food chopper. Add suet which has been chopped fine, brown sugar, currants, and raisins which have been washed and drained, apples and other fruits. If you have a jar of syrup from peach pickles, do by all means use it for part of liquid. Cook over a low fire until the apples are tender, seal in sterile jars. It is now ready for pies.

SNITZ FOR PIE

¾ bushel apples
12 c. white sugar
4 T. cinnamon

2 T. allspice
2 t. salt
5 heaping T. flour or
   cornstarch

Peel apples and put through grinder. Let stand overnight. Stir a few times in the evening so they will not get brown. Next morning add sugar, spices, and salt. Mix well. Add flour mixed with a little water and pour over apples. Stir and mix well. Put in jars and cold pack 1 hour. This should fill a 13 qt. mixing bowl so use apples accordingly.

GRAPE JUICE

12 c. water
12 c. white sugar

6 c. grapes, Concord are
   best

Cook together 5 min. Put through cloth in colander or in a bag to drain. Cold pack for 15 min.

GRAPE JUICE CONCENTRATE

grapes   sugar

Remove grapes from stems and wash thoroughly. Cover with water and heat slowly to simmering until fruit is very soft and most of the skins have come off. Strain through a bag and add ½ c. sugar to each quart of juice. Pour into jars to within ½ inch from top of jar. Tightly place caps and simmer jars for 30 min. in hot bath. DO NOT BOIL. If you don't add sugar you can make jelly later.

EASY GRAPE JUICE

Concord grapes   water
sugar

Put 1½ c. grapes in quart jars. Add ¾ c. sugar to each jar. Fill with water and seal. Cold pack for 20 min.

V-8 JUICE

6 qt. tomato juice   2 t. celery salt
2/3 c. sugar   2 t. onion salt
1 t. garlic salt   2 t. salt

Mix all together. Bring to a boil. Put in jars. Cold pack for 10-15 min.

ROOT BEER

2 c. white sugar   3 t. root beer extract
1 gal. lukewarm water   1 t. dry yeast

Use some hot water to dissolve yeast. Mix together. Put in jars and set in sun for 4 hours. Chill for 24 hours.

Canning Beets & Pickles

PICKLED RED BEETS

2 c. granulated sugar
2 c. vineager - prefer
   apple cider vinegar
2 c. water
1 t. allspice

1 t. cinnamon
1 t. cloves
1 t. celery seeds

First wash and cook beets until tender. Let set until cooled and then peel beets and cut into little squares; bite size. Pour your vinegar, sugars, and ingredients over beets and simmer for 15 min. Pack in heated jars and put on lids and rings. Set jars upside down to seal.

BREAD & BUTTER PICKLES

5 c. white sugar
1½ t. tumeric
2 t. mustard seed

1 t. celery seed
¾ c. vinegar
4 c. water

Slice thin 1 gal. raw cucumbers and 4 small onions. Mix ½ c. salt with them and let stand for 3 hours. Combine and add what's listed up above. Heat and put in jars and seal. Makes 7 pints.

BREAD & BUTTER PICKLES

1 gal. thinly sliced cucumbers
8 sm. onions

½ c. salt

Slice cucumbers and onions; then mix with salt. Cover with water and let set for 3 hours. Drain well and add the following:

5 c. white sugar
1½ t. tumeric

2 T. mustard seed
3 c. vinegar

Bring to a boil and then put in jars. Cold pack for 5 min.

COUISER PICKLES

1/8 t. Alum
7 garlic buds
14 heads dill, for each jar

1 qt. vinegar
1 c. salt
3 qts. water

Place first 3 ingredients in 7 jars. Fill with pickles, bring next 3 ingredients to a boil. Pour over pickles and cover with grape leaf. Put lids on and cold pack to boiling point. Remove. Makes 7 quarts.

SWEET DILL PICKLES

1 qt. vinegar
1 pt. water
4 c. white sugar
¼ c. salt
4 onions, sliced & chopped

Cook this together a few minutes then fill 5 quart jars with sliced pickles. Put 3 little garlic seeds in each jar then pour hot vinegar mix over pickles. Cold pack for 5 min. This is very good.

CANNING SWEET PEPPERS

peppers
cooking oil
salt

Syrup:
1 qt. vinegar
1 c. water
3 c. sugar

Cut peppers in desired sizes and cover with water. Bring to a boil. Drain, put into jars. Add 1 t. oil and 1 t. salt to each jar. Make syrup of vinegar, water, and sugar. Bring to a boil and pour over peppers. Cold pack 5 min.

CINNAMON STICK PICKLES

Peel, seed, and slice pickles to make 2 gal. sticks. Put in crock with **2 c. pickling lime and enough water to cover.** Soak for 24 hours. Drain and wash. Soak again in plain water for 4 hours. Drain and cover with following: **1 c. vinegar, 1 T. alum, ½ bottle red food coloring, and water to cover.** Simmer for 2 hours and throw away liquid.

Cook together **1 T. salt, 2 c. vinegar, 2 c. water, 12 oz. pkg. red cinnamon candy, and 10 c. white sugar.** Bring to a boil and pour over cooked pickles. Let stand for 24 hours. Drain and bring syrup to a boil again. Pour over pickles. Do this for 4 days. Then drain and pack into jars. Heat the syrup to a boil again and pour into jars. Cold pack for 10 min. Very good!

SWEET GARLIC DILL PICKLES

2 heads of dill	2 c. water
pickles	2 T. salt
2 or 3 garlic heads	3 c. sugar
2 c. vinegar	

Put 2 heads of dill in a quart jar. Then slice full of dill size pickles and top with 2 or 3 garlic heads. Heat vinegar, water, salt, and sugar. Bring this to a boiling point and pour over pickles. Cold pack just to boiling point. Don't let it boil. Remove jars right away.

SWEET DILLS

Heat:

3 c. sugar	1 c. vinegar
3 c. water	1 T. salt

Wash and slice cucumbers. Put 1 sprig dill, 1 clove garlic, and cucumbers into quart jars. Cover with hot syrup. Cold pack until water boils, then turn off heat. Let jars set in water until cooled. Do not open until aged 1 month.

LIME PICKLES

Slice 7 lbs. pickles. Put in **2 c. pickling lime and 2 gal. cold water.** Let stand overnight then rinse 3 times. Put in cold water for 3 hours, drain, then put in solution of **2 qt. vinegar (scant), 4½ lbs. white sugar, 2 T. salt, 2 t. pickling spice, 1 t. whole cloves, and 1 t. mustard seed**, tie spice in a cloth. Simmer 30 min. then put in hot jars and seal.

GARLIC DILL PICKLES

dill heads	2 c. vinegar
garlic buds	3 t. salt
cucumbers	3 c. sugar

Place 2 heads of dill in a quart jar. Fill jar with cucumbers. Place 2 - 3 garlic buds on top. Bring to a boil the last three ingredients. Then pour over pickles enough to cover. Cold pack just to boiling point. DO NOT BOIL. Remove jars from water right away. Makes 3 quarts.

STUFFED MINI RED PEPPERS

1 c. brown sugar
2 c. vinegar
1 t. celery seed

½ t. mustard
½ t. tumeric
½ t. salt

Stuff peppers with shredded cabbage, place into pint jars. Heat remaining ingredients to a boil. Pour over stuffed peppers in jars. Cold pack for 15 min.

PICKLING YELLOW BEANS

Blanch beans and drain water off. Boil **2 c. vinegar, 2 c. water, and 1½ c. sugar.** Put beans in jars and pour hot vinegar solution over beans. Seal.

PICKLED RED BEETS

beets
4 c. water
4 c. sugar

1 c. vinegar
1 T. salt

Thoroughly wash the beets then boil with skin on until soft. Save the beet juice. Slip skins off and cut into desired sizes. Put in jars. Bring to a boil water, sugar, vinegar, and salt. Pour over beets in jars. Seal and cold pack for 15 min.

MIXED VEGETABLE PICKLES

1 lg. head cauliflower, cut in pcs.
1 qt. small pickles
1 qt. whole small onions
1 qt. celery, diced
2 red sweet peppers, chopped
2 green peppers, chopped
1 qt. carrots, cut in inch pcs.

1 qt. lima beans, or other beans
1 qt. vinegar
2 c. sugar or more to taste
2 T. salt
4 T. dry mustard
2 T. celery seed

Cook each vegetable separately in salt water until just barely tender. Mix cooked vegetables lightly. Combine sugar, salt, mustard, and celery seed and bring to a boil. Add vegetables and reheat. Cold pack for 10 min. after they are in jars.

MIXED PICKLES

2 qt. sm. lima beans
2 qt. lg. lima beans
1 qt. carrots, sliced
1 qt. kidney beans
2 head cauliflower
1 qt. celery, sliced
2 qt. pickles

1 qt. onions, chopped
1 qt. string beans
6 each, red, yellow, and
   green peppers, chopped
   or sliced

Cut up vegetables seperately. Cook each in salt water until tender. Drain and put in cold water and drain again. Add cooked shell macaroni. Put spices in cheese cloth and cook in vinegar mix.

Spices: 2 t. celery seed, 2 cinnamon sticks, and 1 T. pickling spices. Vinegar Mix: 5 c. sugar, 2 c. vinegar, 4 c. water, 2 T. tumeric, and 1 T. clear jel. Remove spices and vegetables in jars. Fill with vinegar mix. Seal and cold pack for ½ hour.

Canning Relishes
& Spreads

SALSA

20 lg. tomatoes	6 T. white sugar
4 lg. onions	1 t. black pepper
4 carrots, grated	3 T. basil
30 sweet Banana peppers	2 T. salt
½ c. parsley, chopped	1 t. cumin
3 hot peppers	1 T. lemon juice

Cut tomatoes, onions, and peppers into chunks. Put in lg. kettle and add rest of ingredients. Cook for 2 hours then put in pint jars and cold pack for 40 min.

SALSA

12 lbs. tomatoes, peeled	4 T. vinegar
4 c. onions, diced	16 jalapeno peppers
4 T. garlic	pickling salt to taste
4 T. cilantro	

Saute onions and garlic. Add peppers and stir 3 to 4 min. Add tomatoes and seasonings. Cook until tomatoes are cooked through. Cold pack for 45 min. Thicken slightly with Clear Jell. May add some green peppers insted of so many jalapeno peppers. I also add a little white sugar.

SALSA

12 lbs. tomatoes, peeled & diced	4 T. vinegar
4 c. onions, diced	16 jalapeno peppers, or less
4 T. garlic, diced	pickling salt to taste
4 t. cilantro	¾ c. sugar

In lg. kettle, saute onion in garlic. Add peppers and stir for 3 to 4 min. Add tomatoes and seasonings. Cook until tomatoes are cooked through. Add sugar. Cold pack for 45 min. Yield: 15 pints

NACHO CHEESE SAUCE

3 (2 lb.) boxes Velveeta cheese
3½ c. cream
¼ lb. butter

1 qt. milk
hot peppers

Melt butter in med. saucepan, then add milk and cream. Slice cheese into mixture. Melt slowly and put in jars. Cold pack for 20 min. Makes 13 pints.

HOT PEPPER MIX (SALSA)

36 hot peppers
15 med. onions
tomato juice

2½ c. sugar
2½ c. vinegar
1 T. salt

Grind pepper and onions (if wanted extra hot, leave in seeds) and put in 4 qt. saucepan. Add tomato juice to cover peppers. Add rest of ingredients and cook for 1 hour. Thicken with Clear Jel. Pour in jars and seal. Also great for hot dogs and hamburgers.

CHEESE WHIZ TO CAN

3 (2 lb.) blocks Velveeta cheese
3½ c. Milnot milk or cream

1 qt. milk
¼ lb. margarine or butter

Melt together over low heat, stirring constantly. Fill pint jars and cold pack for 20 min. Makes 20 pints. *For variation add chopped peppers (hot or mild) before canning.*

HOT PEPPERS

peppers
½ t. salt
1 clove garlic
1 t. salad oil
} per jar

Syrup:
2 c. water
2 c. sugar
2 c. vinegar

Prepare peppers, dice and place into any size jar. Add salt, garlic, and salad oil. Over all this pour syrup. Cold pack until boiling. Let set in water for 5 min. then remove.

ZUCCHINI RELISH

10 c. coarsely chopped zucchini	5 T. salt
4 c. coarsely chopped onions	

Mix these ingredients and let stand overnight. Next day drain and rinse twice. Then add these ingredients:

2½ c. vinegar	1 t. dry mustard
4 c. peppers	1 t. celery seed
4 c. sugar	1 t. tumeric
1 t. nutmeg	1 t. black pepper

Mix all together and cook for 30 min. Put into hot jars and seal.
Yield: 10 pints

PEPPER RELISH

12 red peppers	12 onions
12 green peppers	

Grind together fine with the food grinder. Pour boiling water over it until covered. Let stand for 15 min. Then drain and add:

1 qt. vinegar	2 T. salt
5 c. white sugar	2 oz. mustard seed

Cook for 20 min. Put in jars and seal.

SANDWICH SPREAD

6 green tomatoes	1 onion
6 peppers all colors	

Grind together and drain. Add ½ c. mustard, ½ c. vinegar, 1½ c. white sugar, and ½ T. celery seed. Boil 10 min. Then add: ½ c. flour. Bring to a boil. Remove from heat and stir in 1 pint salad dressing and can it.

HOT DOG RELISH

36 mild or hot peppers	2½ c. sugar
15 med. onions	2½ c. vinegar
tomato juice	1 T. salt

Grind peppers and onions and put in lg. sauce pan. Add tomato juice enough to cover peppers and onions. Then add rest of ingredients and cook for 1 hour. Thicken with ½ cup clear jel and add water slowly until watery. Then add to pot, stirring in slowly. Put in jars and cold pack for 25 min.

CUCUMBER RELISH

6 lg. cucumbers
4 lg. onions
4 lg. peppers
2 T. salt
1 T. celery seed

1 T. mustard seed
½ t. tumeric
2 c. vinegar
5 c. sugar
2 drops green coloring

Grind cucumbers, onions, and peppers. Mix in salt and let set overnight. Drain and rinse. Add remaining ingredients. Cook slowly until thick and most of juice has boiled away. Approximately 30 to 40 min. Pack in sterilized jars. Yield: 3 pints.

SANDWICH SPREAD

6 lg. onions
6 green tomatoes

6 red peppers
6 green peppers

Grind, mix in **1 lg. T. salt**. Let drain for 1 hour. Put in **1 qt. vinegar, 1 qt. water**, and boil 15 min. Add **1 c. flour, 5 c. white sugar, 1 T. tumeric, and 1 pint mustard**. Boil 5 min. Put in jars and seal.

GREEN TOMATO RELISH

24 green tomatoes
6 green peppers
12 onions
1 red pepper

6 c. white sugar
2 T. salt
1 pint vinegar
½ c. mixed whole spices in
bag

Grind together the first 4 ingredients and drain. Mix in the rest of the ingredients. Boil together for 20 min. Remove bag and seal relish in jars.

SANDWICH SPREAD

3 c. sugar
6 lg. pickles
6 green tomatoes
6 lg. onions
6 green peppers
6 red peppers
1 pt. vinegar
1 can Carnation milk
1 jar French prepared mustard

1 T. tumeric
1 c. flour
½ c. butter
1 t. mustard seed
1 t. celery seed
2 eggs
1 stalk celery
salt to taste

Put pickles, tomatoes, onions, and peppers through a food grinder. Place in a large kettle and cook with half of sugar for 30 min. Add remaining ingredients and heat to boiling. Put in jars and cold pack 10 minutes.

PICANTE SAUCE

12 c. cubed & peeled tomatoes
5 lg. onions
9 hot peppers
2 bell peppers

¾ c. sugar
¼ c. salt
1 c. vinegar
1 c. tomato paste

Grind peppers and onions; mix together with tomatoes and remaining ingredients. Cook 30 min. Cold pack for 30 min. Yield: 6 - 8 pt.

PEACH JAM

6 c. peaches, chopped
6 c. white sugar

2 c. crushed pineapples

Cook together 20 min. Add 6 oz. orange jello. Put in jars and seal or cold pack a few minutes.

APPLE BUTTER

3 gal. apple slices, not cooked
8 lbs. white sugar

½ gal. dark Karo
1 gal. light Karo

Cook slowly for 4 hours. Put lid on until it cooks. Put through sieve and add 1½ t. cinnamon. Put in jars and cold pack for 10 min. Makes 3 gallons.

APPLE BUTTER MADE ON STOVE

4 gals. sour snitz   1 gal. dark Karo
4 lbs. white sugar

Put Karo and sugar in lard can or something with a tight lid. Mix sugar and syrup well before putting apples in. Put on aseptic pad and boil for 3 hours without opening. Then put through sieve and add vinegar and spices to taste. If you do not open before time, the apples will stay on top.

ZUCCHINI JAM

6 c. grated, peeled zucchini   1 (8 oz.) crushed pineapple
6 c. white sugar   1 (6 oz.) pkg. orange jello
2 T. Realemon

Boil zucchini for 6 min. Add sugar, Realemon, and pineapple. Boil 6 more minutes, add jello. Put in jars and seal. Cold pack for 8 min.

RED BEET JELLY

9 beets   8 c. sugar
6 c. beet juice   1 (6 oz.) pkg. red raspberry
2 pkg. Sure Jel   jello
½ c. lemon juice

Wash beets well, cook until done. Make sure to have 6 cups juice. (Use juice only, not beets.) Mix together beet juice, Sure Jel, and lemon juice. Bring to a boil and add sugar and jello. Boil for 6 min. Pour into glass jars and seal. Cold pack for 5 min.

RHUBARB JAM

5 c. rhubarb   5 c. sugar

Let soak overnight. Cook 5 min. then add 2 (3 oz.) boxes strawberry jello. Add 1 c. water. Put in jars, cold pack for 5 min.

HOMEMADE HONEY

5 lbs. white sugar **1½ pt. water**

Boil until clear. Add **1 t. alum**. Remove from stove then add 85 red clover blossoms or 100 white blossoms. Let stand 10 min. Strain out blossoms. Tastes like honey.

CORN COB SYRUP

6 red corn cobs, washed **3 qt. water**
3 lbs. brown sugar

Break corn cobs in pieces. Boil in water for 1 hour. Strain and add sugar and water enough to make 3 qt. Boil until it starts to thicken or consistency of maple syrup. Be sure to select clean cobs free from mold. Light colored cobs make a lighter syrup and give better flavor. Tastes just as good as maple syrup.

PEACH HONEY

7 c. sugar **1 small can crushed**
6 c. mashed peaches **pineapple**

Cook all together for 20 min. Put in hot jars and seal or freeze.

ELDERBERRY PRESERVES

½ gal. light Karo **1 qt. juice**
½ gal. white sugar

Cook for 10 to 15 min. Put in jars and seal. Cold pack for 8 min.

ORANGE PINEAPPLE PRESERVES

2 c. crushed pineapple **1 orange, (cut up in thin**
2 c. light Karo **slices, including rind)**

Heat sugar and Karo until boiling. Add pineapple and orange. Bring to rolling boil. Boil for 2 min.

GRAPE BUTTER

1 qt. grapes (whole)   2 T. water
1 qt. sugar

Cook for 20 min. then put through food mill or blender. Put in jars and seal.

STRAWBERRY BANANA JAM

4¾ c. strawberries, mashed   6¾ c. sugar
3 fully ripe bananas   1 box Sure Jel (fruit pectin)
3 T. fresh lemon juice   ½ t. butter

Measure fruit in 6 - 8 qt. sauce pot. Add 1½ c. bananas. Stir in lemon juice; measure sugar into bowl. Stir Sure Jel into fruit in saucepan; add butter. Bring mixture to full rolling boil, and boil exactly 1 min. stirring constantly. Remove from heat, skim off foam with metal spoon. Ladle quickly into hot sterilized jars. Put on lids and screw tightly. Invert jars 5 min. then turn upright.

APPLE BUTTER

4 gals. apples, peeled & cored   1 t. cinnamon
6 lbs. sugar   1 t. allspice
1 gal. Karo syrup   1 pint vinegar

Put everything in canner and let stand overnight. Next morning cook over low heat for 3 hours. Don't uncover or it will scorch. Put in pint jars and cold pack for 10 min.

RHUBARB JAM

5 c. rhubarb   1 pkg. strawberry jello
3 c. sugar   1 pkg. strawberry Kool-aid

Mix rhubarb and sugar. Let stand overnight. Cook until rhubarb is tender. Add jello and Kool-Aid. Put in jars and seal. Cold pack for 5 min.

ORANGE MARMALADE

2 c. finely chopped orange peels   **1½ qt. water**
1 qt. chopped orange pulp   **6 c. sugar**
1 c. chopped fine lemon, fresh

Mix all ingredients except sugar and simmer for 8 min. Cover and let set for 16 hours in a cool place. Cook for 1 hour or until peelings are tender. Add 1 c. sugar for each cup mixture, stir until sugar is dissolved. Cook on high heat to gelling point. Stir at all times. Put in jars and leave ¼ inch head space. Put on lids and cold pack for 10 min. Makes about 7 half pints.

HOMEMADE SOAP

4½ lbs. lard   **1 can lye**
3 qt. cold water

Put lard in granite or stainless steel bowl. Add lye water a little at a time, keep stirring until dissolved. Stir until it thickens like gravy. Takes about 15 min. of stirring. Set it aside. Cut in bars after a few days.

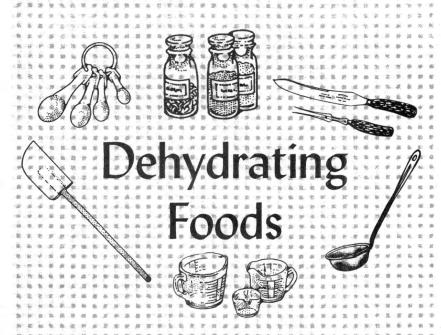

Dehydrating
Foods

DRYING VEGETABLES

Vegetables usually take between 3 to 14 hours. Generally it takes 15 min. to 3 hours for rehydration depending on the texture and thickness of vegetables.

ONIONS

Use white or yellow variety. Large pungent varieties dry best. Cut off ends and peel. Dice into small pieces. Dry at 140° until brittle. Use in soups or casseroles. Or grind to make onion powder for seasoning.

PEAS

Shell and wash peas, steam blanch for 3 min. Dry at 125° F until crisp. Good in soups.

SWEET POTATOES OR YAMS

Use thick orange potatoes free from blemishes. Peel and cut into ¼ inch slices. Steam blanch for 3½ min. Dry at 125° F until brittle. Good for candied yams or to bake in pies and breads.

TOMATOES

Use Roma or other paste type tomato. Wash and dip in boiling water for 45 seconds, then dip in cold water and remove skins. Cut into thin slices. Dry at 145° F until crispy. Use for soups, sauces, or can be powder to thicken other tomato sauces.

ZUCCHINI

Use young, tender, slender zucchinis, wash and cut into thin slices. Dry at 125° until brittle. Good in soups, casseroles, or sprinkle zucchini chips with seasoned salt and serve as chips. Or serve with dip.

POTATOES

Use any white variety, wash well to remove dirt. Peel and cut into ¼" thick slices. Steam blanch 6 min. Rinse well in cold water to remove all starch. Dry on racks at 125° until crisp. Good for soups, casseroles, or season and eat as chips Fat Free.

PARSLEY, BASIL, OREGANO, TEA LEAVES

Cut fresh from garden in morning or evening and wash. Then dry on paper towels; put on cookie sheets and dry in oven at lowest setting until brittle. Put in canning jars to store.

ASPARAGUS

Choose young tender stalks and cut off tough end. Slice into 1 inch pieces. Steam blanch for 4 min. Dry at 120° until brittle. Use in soups or with seasoned cream sauce.

BEANS - GREEN OR YELLOW

Choose a variety with thick walls, crisp and with small seeds. Wash and snap off ends, cut diagonally into 1 inch pieces or use frencher. Steam blanch 4 - 6 min. Put beans in freezer for 30 min. Dry at 125° F until brittle. Use in casseroles, soups, or stews.

CARROTS

Choose deep orange mature variety. Trim off tops and peel. Slice crosswise or dice finely. Steam blanch for 3 min. Dry at 125° F until almost brittle. Use in soups or stews, or grate before drying to use in cakes or muffins.

CORN OR CORNMEAL

Choose any yellow variety with tender sweet kernels. Husk corn, remove silk and wash. Steam until milk is set. Cool. Carefully cut corn from cob with sharp knife. Dry at 125° F until brittle. Good in soups, chowder, fritters, or grind to make cornmeal.

MUSHROOMS

Choose only edible cultivated mushrooms with small closed caps. Wash to remove dirt. Slice into thin slices. Dry at 125° F until brittle. Good in soups and casserole.

BEEF JERKEY

3 lb. lean beef (round sirloin tip or flank steak are good)

¾ c. soy sauce	1 clove garlic, crushed
½ c. Worcestershire sauce	½ t. cracked pepper
¼ c. brown sugar	½ t. liquid smoke
¼ c. salt	2 c. water
1 t. onion powder	

Cut beef across the grain into ½ inch thick strips. Combine all ingredients. Add beef cover and refrigerate overnight. Drain and dry in electric dehydrator at 145° until pliable. Or smoke in smoker with hickory chips until pliable. Store in food storage bags or canning jars.

APPLES

apples, buy any firm textured apple

Wash, core, and peel apples. Cut into small thin slices or into rings. Dip in lemon juice. Dry at 130° until pliable. Use as snack or in oatmeal, or for baking pies or cobblers, etc.

APRICOTS

firm apricots

Wash and cut in half. Remove pits and peel and slice. Put on trays. Dry at 135° until pliable with no moisture pockets. Use for snacks, or in oatmeal, salads, or good to add to nut bread.

BANANAS

Buy slightly brown, speckled yellow variety. Peel and cut into ¼" slices. Dip in lemon juice. Dry at 130° until pliable or almost crisp. Very good in cakes, cereal, or snacks.

BLUEBERRIES

Coose large firm blueberries. Wash and remove stems. Put in boiling water for ½ min. Drain well. Put on trays and dry at 135° until leathery appearance. Eat like raisins or in breads or cakes.

CHERRIES

Buy sweet cherries for snacks or cereals. Buy sour cherries for baking. Cut in half, remove pits and dry at 160° for 2½ hours. Then dry at 135° F until leathery.

COCONUTS

Buy fresh coconuts, heavy and full of milk. Pierce eyes to remove milk. Crack open shell with hammer and cut out coconut meat. Thinly slice or grate. Dry at 130° F until crisp. Use for baking or good as a snack.

GRAPES

Buy red seedless or Thompsons. Wash and remove stems. Dip in boiling water for 45 seconds. Drain and put on trays. Dry at 130° F until pliable like raisins.

PEACHES

Use Freestone or Chinastone, ripe and firm. Dip in boiling water for 1 min. then dip in cold water. Slip off peels and cut in half. Remove stones. Cut into ½" thick slices. Dip in lemon juice and put on trays. Dry at 135° F until pliable.

PEARS

Use ripe pears any kind. Wash, peel, and core. Slice into ½" pieces. Dip into lemon or lime juice. Put on trays and dry at 130° F until leathery. Very good snack.

PINEAPPLES

Buy fully ripe pineapples with yellowish brown peels. Peel and core, cut into ½" slices. Put on trays and dry at 135° until leathery and not sticky. Very good snack or use in baking.

PRUNE PLUMS

Ripe prune plums are slightly soft with sweet flesh. Cut in half and remove pits. Push against the peel part to expose more of pulp surface to dry. Dry peel side down at 130° until soft and pliable.

FRUIT LEATHER

apples, can use applesauce	cherries
peaches	pears
apricots	pineapples
berries	plums

All can be fresh, frozen, or canned.

Wash all fresh fruits and peel, or use canned or frozen. Puree fruits in blender or food processor until smooth. Add honey or bananas for sweetness if desired. If too thick add fruit juice. Bring to a boil if using fresh or frozen apples, peaches, or pears. Cover trays with heavy food grade plastic wrap. Or specifically designed sheets that come with most dehydrators. Or use cookie sheets if using oven. Spread puree evenly, about 1/8 inch thick. Dry at 125° F until leathery texture. Cut into strips and roll up and wrap each piece individually. Good for a snack.

TRAIL MIX

½ c. each almonds, dried apples, dried apricots, dried bananas, coconut chips, dried pears, dried pineapple, raisins, sunflower seeds, chocolate chips if desired

Mix all together and store in canning jars, food bags, or sealed containers.

GREEN BEANS WITH HAM

2 c. dried green beans
2½ c. boiling water
2 T. butter or margarine
¼ c. chopped onion
¼ c. chopped celery
½ c. diced cooked ham
salt and pepper (opt.)

Reconstitute dried green beans in boiling water. Let stand about 1 hour. Melt butter in a lg. saucepan. Saute onions and celery until soft, do not brown. Add ham and cook for 2 to 3 minutes. Add green beans and liquid. Simmer, uncovered for about 30 to 40 min. Additional water may be added. Season with salt and pepper if desired.

CORN CHOWDER

1 c. dried corn
4 c. boiling water
½ c. celery, chopped
¼ c. onion, chopped
1/8 c. green pepper, diced
½ c. bacon, fried & crumbled
1 c. peeled, chopped potato
1/8 t. salt
1/8 t. pepper
2½ c. milk

Rehydrate corn in 2 c. boiling water. Let set for 2½ hours. Saute celery, onion, and green pepper in bacon grease until tender. Add potatoes, rest of water, 2 c. salt, and pepper. Simmer for 45 min. Add corn, liquid and milk. Simmer for another 30 min. Then add bacon.

GRANOLA

4 c. uncooked oatmeal
½ c. wheat germ
1 c. coconut
1 c. slivered almonds
1 c. sunflower seeds
½ c. honey

¼ c. olive oil
½ c. brown sugar
1 t. vanilla
1 t. cinnamon
1 c. raisins
salt

Combine all ingredients except raisins. Mix well, spread on cookie sheet. Bake at 300° F for half hour, stirring every 10 min. Mixture can also be dried in electric dehydrator at 145° for 3 hours. Stir in raisins.

CHEESY POTATOES

3 c. dried potatoes
3 c. boiling water
1½ c. Cheddar or Colby cheese, grated

¾ c. milk, heated
1 t. salt
1/8 t. pepper
2 T. butter

Butter casserole dish, place dried potatoes in bottom. Cover with boiling water. Let set for 3 min. Add 1 c. cheese, milk, salt, and pepper. Bake at 350° covered for 35 min. Remove from oven and add remaining cheese cover and bake another 25 min.

BANANA NUT BREAD

1 c. dried bananas
1 c. water
1¾ c. flour
2¼ t. baking powder
½ t. salt

1/3 c. butter
½ c. sugar
2 eggs, beaten
½ c. chopped walnuts

Rehydrate bananas in 1 c. water. Let stand 1 hour. Grease a 9 x 5 x 3 inch loaf pan. Sift together flour, baking powder, and salt. Cream butter, sugar, and add dry ingredients. Stir in bananas, nuts, and eggs. Blend, pour batter into loaf pan. Bake at 350° for 1 hour or until done.

VEGGIE QUICHE

½ c. dried veg. (corn, peas, onions, green beans, carrots, etc.)
½ c. boiling water   salt & pepper to taste
2 c. creamer milk   9 inch pastry for single
3 eggs   crust pie
½ c. shredded Swiss cheese

Rehydrate veggies in boiling water. Let set for 1½ hours or until vegetables are soft. Drain, whip together milk, eggs, salt, and pepper. Stir in veggies and pour mix into a prepared pie shell. Sprinkle with cheese. Bake at 375° for 35 to 40 min. or until filling is set.

CHICKEN DUMPLIN'S

1½ c. dried vegetables (peas, potatoes, carrots, celery, onion, & parsley
2 c. chicken chunks   1 c. milk
2 c. chicken broth   3 T. flour
4 c. water   2 c. Bisquik
2 T. chicken soup base   ¾ c. milk
salt & pepper to taste

Add 2 c. boiling water to vegetables. Let set for 1 hour. Add chicken broth, water, soup base, salt, pepper. Simmer for half hour. Mix together flour and milk, mix well. Blend into rest of ingredients. Mix together Bisquik and milk. Drop by T. into bubbling gravy. Cover and let simmer for half an hour or until done. Serve over rice biscuits.

INDEX

Harvest Time

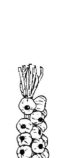

'Tis canning time far and wide
Across this whole vast countryside.
They're carrying empties from below
Or toting full jars down to stow.
Mom has a feeling it's all right
To bottle everything in sight.
Our meals are lean and hurried up
While Mom fills up her measuring cup -
With beans or peas or carrots gold,
She knows next winter will be cold.
For these past months about everywhere
There's not a single inch to spare.
There's jars of beets and jars of corn
A-gathering there since early morn -
There's relish pickles, catsup, and jam
In fact as much as Mom could ram.
In jars of every shape and size
That she could really utilize
Mom says it isn't right to waste
What God provides, so she makes haste;
From summertime till late in fall
The vegetables are in our own lot
And everything the neighbors got.
Our porch and kitchen overflow
And keep us running to and fro -
With baskets full of everything
That has been grown since early spring.
There's running to the country store
For rubber rings and lids, and more
For spices, sugar, salt, and wax
And won't let Dad and me relax.

Cont.'d on next page

There's pickles fat, and pickles lean
And every kind of long stringbean.
There's peas and white and yellow corn
That Dad and I have meekly borne -
From garden, patch, and berry row
And everywhere that we did hoe...
Oh, well our cellars's nearly full
And I mean really bountiful
And Mom's as happy as can be
That she went on the canning spree
And I must own I really love
The smell of cinnamon and clove...
Of vinegar and spicy pears
And all the juices Mom prepares...
There's charm to canning time each year
With canning's special atmosphere.
But we know Mom; we know her mind
For she is merciful and kind...
Our shelves are loaded down today
But Mom will give about half away!